Blaze the Trail, Snoopy

Selected cartoons from
AND A WOODSTOCK IN A BIRCH TREE
Volume 2

by CHARLES M. SCHULZ

BLAZE THE TRAIL, SNOOPY

This book, prepared especially for Fawcett Crest Books, a
unit of CBS Publications, the Consumer Publishing Division
of CBS Inc., comprises a portion of AND A WOODSTOCK
IN A BIRCH TREE and is reprinted by arrangement with
Holt, Rinehart and Winston, Inc.

Contents of Book: PEANUTS® comic strips by
                  Charles M. Schulz
                  Copyright © 1978 United Feature
                  Syndicate, Inc.

ISBN: 0-449-24452-0

Printed in the United States of America

First Fawcett Crest Printing: October 1981

10 9 8 7 6 5 4 3 2 1

Blaze the Trail, Snoopy

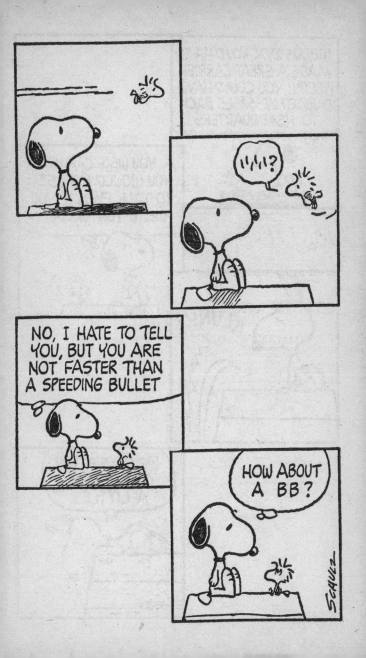

WOODSTOCK, YOU'D HAVE MADE A GREAT CARRIER PIGEON! YOU COULD HAVE CARRIED MESSAGES BACK TO HEADQUARTERS...

IF YOU WERE CAPTURED, YOU WOULD REFUSE TO TALK EVEN IF YOU WERE TORTURED!

KLUNK!

WELL, MAYBE YOU COULD TALK A LITTLE...

Schulz

THERE ARE DIFFERENT WAYS OF TRAINING DOGS

I'VE BEEN READING ABOUT THE "SHAKE AND THROW" METHOD OF TRAINING PUPPIES...

A MOTHER DOG CAN'T HIT A PUPPY SO SHE PICKS IT UP, SHAKES IT AND THEN DROPS IT!

LAST WEEK MY MOTHER SAID TO ME, "EUDORA, I THINK YOU SHOULD GO TO SUMMER CAMP!"

SO HERE I AM IN THE WILDERNESS

IT'S NOT TOO BAD... YOU MAY EVEN LIKE IT...

SO I'LL ASK YOU THE SAME THING I ASKED HER...

WHAT IF I GET EATEN BY AN ANTELOPE?

HEY, EUDORA, WE HAVE TO GO TO THE MAIN HALL FOR ORIENTATION!

IF THEY TRY TO SHIP US TO THE ORIENT, FORGET IT!

HOW DO YOU FEEL ABOUT WASHING DISHES AND SETTING TABLES?

I'D RATHER GO TO THE ORIENT!

IF WE BECAME LOST IN THE WOODS, HOW LONG COULD WE GO WITHOUT REAL FOOD?

I'LL BET WE COULD GO FOR A MONTH WITHOUT REAL FOOD

HOW ABOUT JUNK FOOD?

ELEVEN MINUTES!

YOU'RE GOING TO TAKE ME FISHING? THAT'S GREAT! I DON'T KNOW ANYTHING ABOUT FISHING

WELL, WHAT WE'LL DO IS, WE'LL GO DOWN ON THE DOCK, AND SEE IF THERE ARE ANY FISH IN THE LAKE, AND THEN...

I SEE ONE!

YOU JUST PADDLE AROUND THERE AWHILE, AND I'LL EXPLAIN ABOUT THESE POLES...

OKAY, EUDORA, YOU FISH IN THIS PART OF THE STREAM, AND I'LL FISH DOWN THERE IN THAT PART...

I DON'T THINK THIS IS GOING TO WORK

WHAT'S THE TROUBLE?

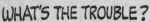

EITHER THE STREAM IS TOO NARROW, OR MY LINE IS TOO LONG...

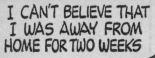

I'VE PLAYED AGAINST "CRYBABY" BOOBIE BEFORE! IT'S AN EXPERIENCE!

HER BROTHER, BOBBY BOOBIE, DOESN'T SAY MUCH, BUT SHE COMPLAINS ABOUT EVERYTHING

JUST DON'T LET HER GET TO YOU....JUST LET IT ALL GO IN ONE EAR AND OUT THE OTHER...

THAT'S THE SPIRIT, PARTNER!

OKAY, WE'LL RECEIVE ON THIS SIDE

THAT'S NOT FAIR!

THAT MEANS WE HAVE THE SUN IN OUR EYES! WHY DO WE ALWAYS SERVE WITH THE SUN IN OUR EYES?!

SEE? DIDN'T I TELL YOU? "CRYBABY" BOOBIE COMPLAINS ABOUT EVERYTHING!

I THINK THE NET IS TOO HIGH! THESE BALLS FEEL DEAD! I CAN'T PLAY ON A SLOW COURT! THESE BALLS ARE TOO LIVELY! I THINK THE NET IS TOO LOW!

HONK!

ALL RIGHT, "CRYBABY," TELL YOUR MOTHER TO CUT IT OUT!

SHE SITS THERE IN HER CAR, AND EVERY TIME YOU MAKE A GOOD SHOT, SHE HONKS THE HORN!

THE NEXT TIME SHE DOES THAT I'M GONNA TEAR OFF A WHEEL!

I COULD HAVE STAYED HOME AND GOTTEN INTO A NICE GENTLE DOGFIGHT

ALL RIGHT, PARTNER, IT'S MATCH POINT...

WE HAVE TO CONCENTRATE! THAT'S THE SECRET, PARTNER! CONCENTRATE!

I GOT A LETTER FROM MY BROTHER, SPIKE, TODAY...

HAS ANYONE EVER NOTICED THAT THE PORTRAIT OF CARL SANDBURG ON A THIRTEEN-CENT STAMP LOOKS LIKE PANCHO GONZALES?

I HAVE AN IDEA

WHY DON'T WE TRY TO FIND A FAMILY AROUND HERE THAT WOULD ADOPT SPIKE?

CAN YOU THINK OF ANY REASON WHY SOMEONE MIGHT NOT WANT HIM?

WELL, HIS BACKHAND IS A LITTLE WEAK...

SCHULZ

YES, WE'RE THE PARTY THAT RAN THE AD IN THE NEWSPAPER...

YES, WE'RE TRYING TO FIND A NICE HOME FOR A DOG..ACTUALLY, HE'S THE BROTHER OF OUR OWN DOG...

OH, NO...HE WOULDN'T BE A LOT OF TROUBLE... NO, HE AMUSES HIMSELF QUITE WELL....

AH, COLONEL HOGAN!

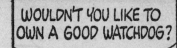

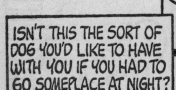

BEETHOVEN NEVER OWNED A DOG

IF BEETHOVEN NEVER OWNED A DOG, I GUESS I SHOULDN'T EITHER..I'M SORRY, CHARLIE BROWN...

BEETHOVEN WOULD HAVE LIKED **THIS** DOG!!

STILL HITTING BALLS WITH THE GARAGE, I SEE...

IT'S GOOD PRACTICE..HE GETS EVERYTHING BACK

I WAS SURPRISED YOU DIDN'T PLAY DOUBLES AT WIMBLEDON THIS YEAR..

THE GARAGE HATES TO FLY

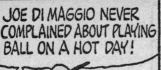

ALL RIGHT, TROOPS... BEFORE WE GO ON OUR HIKE, I'LL CALL THE ROLL

WOODSTOCK! CONRAD! BILL! OLIVIER!

ZZZZ

I SHOULD NEVER CALL THE ROLL BEFORE NOON!

INCIDENTALLY, HOW DO YOU GUYS LIKE THE GRAPE JELLY I BROUGHT ALONG?

IT'S A NEW BRAND CALLED "SMIRK"

IF SOMEONE GETS JELLY ON HIS FACE, YOU CAN SAY TO HIM, "WIPE THAT 'SMIRK' OFF YOUR FACE!"

JUST A LITTLE JOKE THERE TO BOOST SAGGING MORALE

OKAY, MEN, THE HIKE IS OVER... WE'RE HOME!

THIS IS WHERE YOU LIVE...WAKE UP!

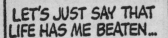

LET'S JUST SAY THAT LIFE HAS ME BEATEN...

SO I GIVE UP! I ADMIT THAT THERE'S NO WAY I CAN WIN...

WHAT IS IT YOU WANT, CHARLIE BROWN?

HOW ABOUT TWO OUT OF THREE?

RIDING AROUND ON THE BACK OF YOUR MOTHER'S BICYCLE IN THE HOT SUN IS NOT MY IDEA OF LIVING...

AT THE END OF THE DAY I FEEL LIKE A FRIED EGG...

THE ONLY THING THAT HELPS IS WHEN SHE ACCIDENTALLY DRIVES US THROUGH A..

...SPRINKLER!

HEY, MANAGER, YOU SHOULD READ THIS BOOK

IT'S CALLED, "WINNING AND TEN OTHER CHOICES"

WHAT ARE THE TEN OTHER CHOICES?

TYING, LOSING, LOSING, LOSING, LOSING, LOSING, LOSING, LOSING, LOSING AND LOSING!

HELLO?
INFORMATION?

YES, I'D LIKE TO TALK
TO A CERTAIN LITTLE
RED-HAIRED GIRL...

NO, I ALREADY HAVE
HER NUMBER...I WAS
HOPING YOU COULD TELL
ME SOMETHING ELSE...

WHAT DO I SAY
WHEN SHE ANSWERS
THE PHONE?

I'LL BET YOU DIALED MY NUMBER BY MISTAKE, DIDN'T YOU, CHUCK? I'LL BET YOU MEANT TO CALL PEPPERMINT PATTY...

SHE JUST HAPPENS TO BE RIGHT HERE BESIDE ME.. I'LL PUT HER ON...

NO! WAIT! I...

HI, CHUCK! FINALLY GOT UP NERVE TO CALL ME, EH?

WHAT DID YOU WANT TO TALK TO ME ABOUT, CHUCK?

IF IT'S ABOUT GOING TO THE SHOW, WHY DON'T WE JUST MEET THERE AROUND ONE? THAT'LL SAVE YOU COMIN' CLEAR OVER HERE!

SEE YOU, CHUCK! GLAD YOU GOT OVER YOUR SHYNESS AND DECIDED TO CALL!

I CAN'T STAND IT...

I JUST SAW SOMETHING I'D LIKE TO HAVE FOR SCHOOL...A FIVE HUNDRED DOLLAR LUNCH BOX!

FIVE HUNDRED DOLLARS?!

THAT'S A LOT OF MONEY TO PAY FOR A LUNCH BOX

BUT WOULDN'T THE SANDWICHES TASTE GREAT?

SCHOOL JUST STARTED AND ALREADY I SHOULD QUIT!

MY TEACHER YELLS AT ME, THE KIDS LAUGH AT ME AND THE PRINCIPAL HATES ME

WHAT ABOUT THE CUSTODIAN?

HE VACUUMED UP MY LUNCH!

YES, MA'AM? YOU WANT ME TO WORK OUT THE PROBLEM AT THE BOARD?

WELL, LET'S SEE.. WE HAVE THESE NUMBERS HERE, DON'T WE?

4678
x 52

THESE ARE NICE NUMBERS, MA'AM..

4,678
x 52

A FOUR, A SIX, A SEVEN, AN EIGHT, A FIVE AND A TWO

OH, YES, AND WE ALSO HAVE AN X...

WELL, THE PROBLEM SEEMS TO BE TO TRY TO FIND OUT WHAT THIS X IS DOING AMONG ALL THESE NUMBERS...

IS HE AN OUT-SIDER? WAS HE INVITED TO JOIN THE GROUP? IT'S AN INTERESTING QUESTION...

LET'S FIND OUT WHAT THE REST OF THE CLASS THINKS... YOU THERE, IN THE THIRD ROW...WHAT DO YOU THINK ABOUT THIS? SPEAK UP!

MA'AM?

RATS! THREE MORE MINUTES AND THE BELL WOULD HAVE RUNG!

SCHULZ

Dear Grandma,
How are you? I am fine.

I have been working
hard in school.

PROBLEM NUMBER SIX...

"HOW MANY GALLONS OF CREAM CONTAINING 25% BUTTER FAT AND MILK CONTAINING 3½% BUTTER FAT MUST BE MIXED TO..

..OBTAIN 50 GALLONS OF CREAM CONTAINING 12½% BUTTER FAT?"

MA'AM, WOULD YOU SETTLE FOR TWENTY PUSH-UPS?

"A Guide to Running"

Chapter One

How to run like a rabbit.

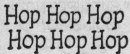

Hop Hop Hop
Hop Hop Hop

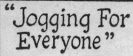
"Jogging For Everyone"

A Detailed Guide to Running

Chapter One

The Left Foot

OH, WELL, IF SOMEONE GIVES YOU A BANANA, I GUESS YOU HAVE TO TRUST HER

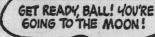

GET READY, BALL! YOU'RE GOING TO THE MOON!

AAUGH!

WHAM!

BANANAS ARE HIGH IN POTASSIUM, CHARLIE BROWN, WHICH PROMOTES HEALING OF MUSCLES!

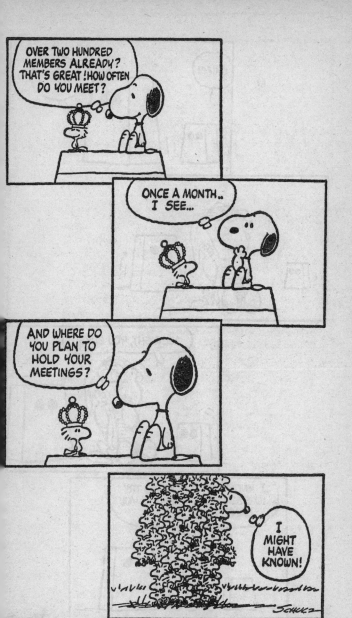

WHAT ARE YOU EATING FOR LUNCH, EUDORA?

THIS IS A CHOCOLATE SANDWICH

I PUT A CHOCOLATE BAR BETWEEN TWO SLICES OF DARK BREAD

I OFTEN WONDER HOW IT WOULD TASTE WITH GRAVY ON IT...

EUDORA! WHAT ARE YOU DOING HERE? THERE'S NO SCHOOL ON SATURDAY!

THERE ISN'T? THAT EXPLAINS EVERYTHING...

SATURDAY'S THE ONLY DAY I NEVER GET ANYTHING WRONG

I WONDER IF IT'S TOO LATE TO BECOME A DISCO...

MORE PEANUTS®

(in editions with brightly colored pages)

☐ A BOY NAMED CHARLIE BROWN	23217	$2.25
☐ SNOOPY AND HIS SOPWITH CAMEL	23799	$1.75
☐ SNOOPY AND THE RED BARON	23719	$1.75
☐ THE "SNOOPY, COME HOME" MOVIE BOOK	23726	$1.95